D0349533

MAD
about

DANCE

JUDITH HENEGHAN

WAYLAND

WAYLAND

First published in 2014 by Wayland
Copyright © Wayland 2014

Wayland
338 Euston Road
London NW1 3BH

Wayland Australia
Level 17/207 Kent Street
Sydney, NSW 2000

All rights reserved

Editor: Nicola Edwards
Design: Rocket Design (East Anglia) Ltd

A catalogue record for this title is available
from the British Library.

ISBN: 978 0 7502 8269 7
Library e-book ISBN: 978 0 7502 8838 5
Dewey number: 792.8-dc23

Printed in China

Wayland is a division of
Hachette Children's Books,
an Hachette UK company

The author and publisher would like to thank the following for allowing their pictures to be reproduced in this publication: Cover: all Shutterstock except (br) Wikimedia Commons; p4 Shuttterstock.com/szefei; p5 (l) Shuttterstock.com/Pavel L Photo and Video, (r) Shuttterstock.com/Jamie Duplass; p6 (t) Shuttterstock.com/Antonio Diaz, (b) Shuttterstock.com/ Syda Productions, p7 (t) Shuttterstock.com/Samuel Borges Photography, (b) Shutterstock.com/Zvonimir Atletic; p8 Luca Di Tommaso / Guinness World Records /Barcroft Media/Barcoft Media via Getty Images; p9 (t) Photo courtesy of the U.S. Department of Defense and Staff Sgt. Timothy Hughes, 75th Fires Brigade (b) Shutterstock.com/Stefano Tinti; p10 Shuttterstock. com/Luis Louro; p11 (t) Getty Images, (b) Shuttterstock.com/ szefei; p12 (t) Shuttterstock.com/Syda Productions, (b) Desiree Navarro/Getty Images; p13 (t) Shutterstock/Netfalls — Remy Musser, (b) Shuttterstock.com/R.Gino Santa Maria; p14 Shuttterstock.com/szefei; p15 (t) Shuttterstock.com/kryzhov, (b) iStock/Getty Images; p16 Denver Post via Getty Images; p17 (tl) iStock/Getty Images, (tr) iStock/Getty Images, (b) Shutterstock. com/Marco Poplasen; p18 Shutterstock.com/Dmitry Morgan; p19 (t) Shutterstock.com/Dmitry Morgan, (m) Shutterstock. com/Dmitry Morgan, (b) Shutterstock.com/Featureflash; p20 WireImage/Getty Images; p21 (t) NBCU Photo Bank via Getty Images, (b) Shutterstock.com/AlenKadr; p22 (t) Shuttterstock. com/Creatista, (b) Getty Images; p23 (t) Shuttterstock.com/ Lorraine Swanson, (b) Shuttterstock.com/ mavkate; p24 (t) Shuttterstock.com/lev radin, (b) Shutterstock.com/Lawrence Wee; p25 (t) Wikimedia Commons, (b) AFP/Getty Images; p26 Shutterstock.com/Kobby Dagan; p27 (t) Shuttterstock. com/DarkBird, (m) Shutterstock.com/Lorraine Swanson, (b) Redferns/Getty Images; p28 (t) Shuttterstock.com/Samuel Borges Photography, (b)Shuttterstock.com/Creatista; p29 (t) Shuttterstock.com/Elena Dijour, (b) Shuttterstock.com/ostill

Every effort has been made to trace the copyright holders. We apologise in advance for any unintentional omissions and would be pleased to insert the appropriate acknowledgements in any future editions of this publication.

Contents

Dance crazy

I love to dance. It doesn't matter where I am – at home, at school, at my dance classes – I'm always tapping my feet, always moving. My mum says I can't sit still. As soon as I hear music, or even when I'm just humming it to myself, I pick up the beat and my energy levels rise. Dancing makes me feel good!

Express yourself

Dance is all about moving expressively to music. This means letting your body respond to the music. All over the world, people use dance to reflect different emotions and there are thousands of different dance styles and traditions. Yet most dancers agree that dancing of any kind is a basic human instinct – just like sleeping or talking.

Separate or together

Dancing can be intensely personal, or a shared experience. Some styles of dance are individual, with the dancer performing a solo or dancing freestyle. Other styles such as ballroom require you to dance with a partner. Several styles such as line dancing involve large groups of dancers all doing the same thing in time to the music. A few styles such as ballet, tap and bhangra may include individual solos, pairs and formation dancing.

So you're not sure if you can dance? Try tapping your foot or clapping to the beat of your favourite music. If you can find the beat, you can dance! Now you all you need are some moves.

top tip

Amy Yakima, winner of the tenth season of US TV show *So You Think You Can Dance* has been dancing since the age of three, when she started studying ballet, tap and jazz. As she got older she added more dance styles such as hip hop to her list. She says: *"I discovered that dance is how I like to communicate. It became my passion. I was at the studio every day, and I loved it."*

THE EXPERT SAYS...

Warm up

Dancing is great exercise. It stretches and strengthens my core muscles as well as being good for my heart and lungs. However, I know I have to warm up first to avoid injury. As well as being painful, a pulled muscle or a strained tendon would mean no dancing while I recover. So I warm up, every time!

This plank stretch helps strengthen abdominal muscles.

Gentle stretches

Start slow, moving your head from side to side and up and down to loosen your neck. Then do some shoulder rolls, followed by body stretches up towards the ceiling and down to your toes. Next, swing your left arm out horizontally to the right across your body, followed by your right arm to the left. Hold each stretch for a count of five.

Get moving

Now do some marching on the spot, starting gently and then raising your knees higher. Take it in turns to point the toe downwards, and then the heel downwards. Finish your warm up with a little light jogging on the spot, or some grapevines. To do a grapevine, take a step to the right, then move your left leg behind your right leg, then your right leg once more to the right before bringing both feet together with a clap. Then do the whole thing in reverse!

CHECKLIST

What to wear?

- ☑ Stretchy clothing
- ☑ Flexible, well-fitting footwear
- ☑ Layers you can remove as you warm up
- ☑ Hair tied back
- ☑ No dangly earrings or necklaces
- ☑ Don't forget to bring plenty of drinking water!

top tip

If the kind of dance you are doing *is* really fast-paced and energetic, like Irish step dancing (right), *it is* important to warm down at the end. Some gentle movements, stretches or walking around will help reduce your heart rate gradually, prevent muscle stiffness and return your body to a restful state.

Line dancing

One way to start dancing is with something simple and sociable, like line dancing. Line dancing is great because you don't need a partner – just a few friends to stand in a line and do some easy steps. My favourite is the Macarena. It's fun at parties because everyone can join in. It also makes a fantastic warm up routine!

The Macarena

Macarena is a Spanish dance song that became really popular in the 1990s. The dance that goes with it has a few basic moves, repeated over and over. As well as the arm movements you can add hip swings and walking on the spot. Its simplicity means big groups of people can join in. In 1996, a crowd of 50,000 people are said to have danced the Macarena at the Yankee Stadium in New York City!

Dancing the Macarena in the Netherlands.

Do the Macarena!

★ *Right arm out in front, palm down*
★ *Left arm out in front, palm down*
★ *Flip your right hand, palm up*
★ *Flip your left hand, palm up*
★ *Right hand on your left shoulder*
★ *Left hand on your right shoulder*
★ *Right hand on your head*
★ *Left hand on your head*
★ *Right arm on your left hip*
★ *Left arm on your right hip*
★ *Right hand on bottom*
★ *Left hand on bottom*
★ *Sway your hips*
★ *Turn to the right with a jump and a clap*
   Repeat!

American line dancing

American line dancing comes from a mix of folk dance and barn dancing. The music is usually country and western and dancers often wear cowboy-style clothing. Dancers stand in a line and the steps are announced and demonstrated by a 'caller' so that everyone knows what to do. Movements focus on the legs — hands are often tucked into the pockets of your jeans!

9

Freestyle

Mix it up

A choreographed dance is one where the moves and steps are designed and practised beforehand. Freestyle means no choreography — dancers improvise with their own moves, often making it up as they go along. Try mixing it up by combining elements of disco, hip hop, salsa or bhangra.
Create your own style.

When me and my friends get together at my house, we always end up dancing. We put on our favourite music and sometimes we make up our own routines or get ideas from YouTube or street dance DVDs. But mostly we just go with the flow! We all have slightly different styles. You've got to dance the way you feel.

A big jump makes a dramatic finish!

THE EXPERT SAYS...

Every time Michael Jackson danced to his own song 'Billy Jean' he included different moves. Although his dancing looked slick and stage-managed, he never danced exactly the same version twice. He once said: *"I just go with the moment ... Performing is not about thinking; it's about feeling."*

Be bold

A confident freestyler will know the music well, be ready for changes in tempo and make several big moves — hands above the head, turning or body popping or shimmying down low. Be bold and get yourself noticed on the dance floor — give it some attitude!

top tip

Some dancers have a few 'signature' moves they use in freestyle dancing – moves that are instantly recognisable as their own. A signature move might be a hand gesture, or a twist, or a pose. Practise one or two of your own, or use a prop such as a hat.

Hip hop and breakdancing

My friend Sam is a great breakdancer. He learned by watching videos and practising over and over. One of his best moves is a 'freeze' where he balances on one hand with his feet in the air. Breakdancing is a bit like gymnastics – you need strength and balance. Sam dances on the pavement but I'd want to practise on a floor mat, first!

Downrocking on the pavement.

Dance with attitude

Street dance is any form of dance that began on the street rather than in a dance studio. Breakdancing, also known as b-boying, is a type of freestyle street dance that emerged in the USA in the 1970s to the sounds of hip hop and funk music. It was made popular by street 'crews' or groups holding dance battles. Dancers showed their creativity and attitude with downrocking (where the shoulders are close to the floor and the hands support the dancer as much as the feet), power moves and freeze poses.

12

Popular techniques

Although breakdancing developed on the street, there are plenty of classes where you can learn some basic moves in safety. Some of the more distinctive elements include popping (jerk-like movements), locking (freezing in position for a second), spinning on the ground using your upper body and, more recently, krumping (intense bursts of movement). Many breakdancing techniques are now mixed into other popular music and dance styles.

top tip

Add some swagger to popular moves like the 'running man' (running on the spot) and the 'sideways shuffle' by using your arms and keeping wrists and hands loose.

CHECKLIST

What do you need?

- ☑ Comfortable, loose clothing
- ☑ A good pair of flexible dance trainers/sneakers – your feet need proper support
- ☑ A gym mat to practise your downrocking drops and moves

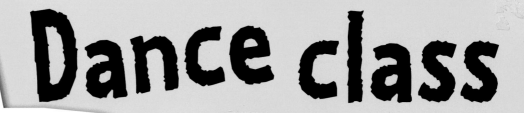

Dance class

I've been going to classes at a local dance studio for the past two years. I started doing ballet when I was eight, and now I'm learning ballroom dancing as well. It's hard work, but fun – at the moment we're practising like mad for a dance show at the end of the month. After class I usually stay on to watch the more advanced dancers. I learn a lot that way.

Learn with others

There are classes for almost every kind of dancing. Your dance teacher will be able to show you the correct positions and techniques; you'll learn with people who are the same standard as you. Classes are a great way to meet other dancers and find dancing partners. You'll also get to hear about dance events and competitions in your area.

THE EXPERT SAYS...

The dancer Martha Graham said that *"Dancing is discovery, discovery, discovery."* Watch yourself in a mirror while you practise. Look up and out rather than down at your feet! Hold your head up high. This creates a more elegant body line and helps you connect with your audience.

The discipline of dance

Many forms of dance use specific techniques, steps and sequences that have developed over decades or even centuries. A video can teach you the steps, but often dance means much more than following a routine. Sometimes it means learning a whole way of moving. Muscles and tendons need to be developed in particular ways; movements should be precise and artistic. A good dance class can help you with this.

top tip

Many dance schools offer free taster sessions. This means you can try out a class to see if you like it. There's so much to choose from!

These dancers are learning a new routine.

Salsa

Learn the basics

Salsa music originated in Cuba with its mix of Spanish and African influences. The Latin American sound travelled to New York where salsa dancing became popular and it is now danced all over the world. There are many different styles of salsa, but the basic step is one step forward and return, then one step back with the other foot and return. Add some rolling hip movement as your weight shifts from foot to foot. Now you can salsa!

Salsa classes are a fantastic way to get into dance. The music is lively and upbeat, you can dance with or without a partner and it's a great way to keep fit and have fun. Like most dances, all you need to get started is a feel for the rhythm. Even my little brother can salsa!

Dance partners run through a salsa routine at a class in Denver, Colorado, USA.

top tip In a salsa step, the ball of the foot usually touches the ground before the heel. Try stepping forwards and backwards in this way, swaying your hips at the same time. Get your arms moving by rolling your shoulders.

Partner up

Dancing with a partner means you can include more complex twists and holds as well as show the 'story' behind the music. One partner takes the lead, and the two can dance in the 'open' or 'closed' positions. 'Open' means dancers hold one or both hands and sometimes move around one another. 'Closed' means the lead dancer puts the right hand on the follower's back, while the follower puts the left hand on the lead's shoulder.

CHECKLIST

Your dance teacher will call out beats from 1-8 as you complete the basic forwards-backwards step.

1 Left foot forward, taking your weight

2 Shift your weight to your right foot

3 Left foot back to starting position

4 Pause

5 Right foot back, taking your weight

6 Shift your weight to your left foot

7 Right foot forward to starting position

8 Pause

open position

closed position

Ballroom

Ballroom dancing includes lots of different dance styles. You always dance with a partner; one leads, the other follows. I started going to ballroom classes a year ago and my teacher gets us to focus on a different dance each month. My favourite so far is the jive. It's fast and the music is really upbeat. I love watching the more experienced dancers do all the twists and spins!

Elegant and poised

Some ballroom dances such as the waltz, the foxtrot and the quickstep focus on grace, elegance and clever footwork to create the appearance of gliding around the dance floor. In competitions, the girls wear floaty dresses and the boys wear smart suits. Dancers always move in an anti-clockwise direction around the floor in a set pattern of steps. This helps prevent collisions!

top ★ tip Ballroom dancing requires some fancy footwork, but the *shoulders* and head must work hard too to maintain the correct posture and poise. When waltzing, hold your tummy in and keep your neck long with shoulders down for a graceful effect. No slouching!

Playful and expressive

Other ballroom dances, often known as Latin, are faster paced, rhythmic, playful and expressive. Examples include the cha cha, rumba, samba, paso doble and jive; the steps allow for more freedom and individuality. In competitions the girls wear shorter skirts and the boys wear tight-fitting trousers to show off their skilled leg movements.

This pair is dancing a fast-paced jive.

The tango comes from Argentina in South America. It's a dramatic dance using both close and open holds. The music has fast sections and slower sections, allowing the dancers to switch mood and vary their steps. The dancers are telling a story through movement.

THE EXPERT SAYS...

Anton du Beke (far right), star of the TV series 'Strictly Come Dancing', began ballroom dancing aged 14. He says: *"It was all about dancing with a partner. That was the key for me. When you dance and it's right – the balance is perfect – it's a moment of perfection."*

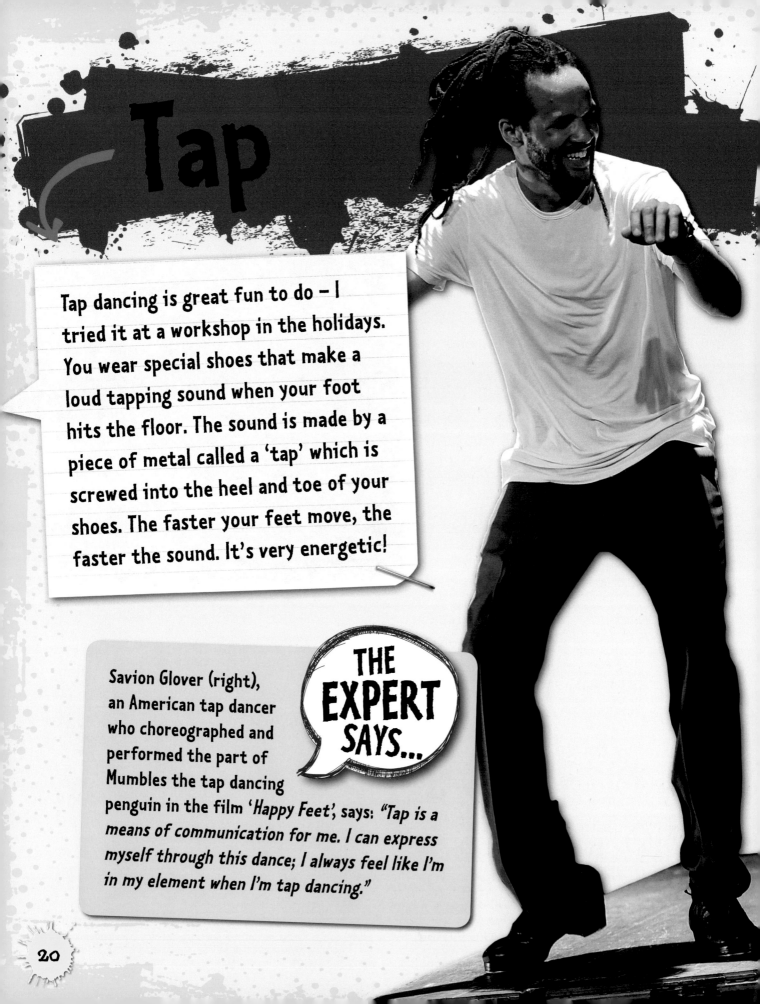

Tap

Tap dancing is great fun to do – I tried it at a workshop in the holidays. You wear special shoes that make a loud tapping sound when your foot hits the floor. The sound is made by a piece of metal called a 'tap' which is screwed into the heel and toe of your shoes. The faster your feet move, the faster the sound. It's very energetic!

THE EXPERT SAYS...

Savion Glover (right), an American tap dancer who choreographed and performed the part of Mumbles the tap dancing penguin in the film 'Happy Feet', says: "Tap is a means of communication for me. I can express myself through this dance; I always feel like I'm in my element when I'm tap dancing."

Sounds and rhythms

Basic steps like a tap with the toe or a tap with the heel create a single sound. Tap dancers combine a variety of toe and heel taps with rapid ankle movements to create more complex sounds and off-beat rhythms known as syncopated rhythms. The different steps have names like stomp, shuffle-hop-step, shimmy and cramp hop.

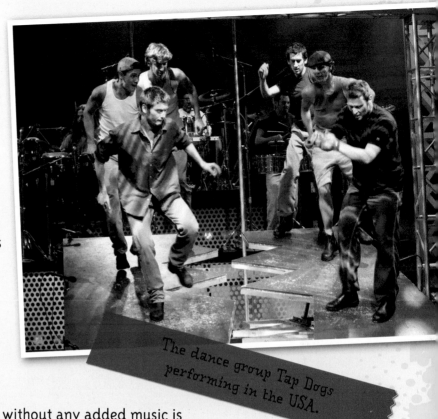

The dance group Tap Dogs performing in the USA.

Broadway style

Tap creates its own sound, and dancing without any added music is called 'a cappella' style. Alternatively you can tap dance to music. This is often called 'Broadway style' and was made popular in the last century by dancers such as Fred Astaire and Gene Kelly, who sang and acted as well. They added aspects of ballroom dancing and even ballet into their skilled and entertaining routines. Nowadays this style is used in musical theatre.

top tip

Different types of tap shoe produce slightly different sounds, or tones. The tone depends on the shape of the tap, its size, and how tightly it is screwed into the shoe. If you don't know what kind of taps to get, check with your teacher.

Ballet

I've been going to ballet classes for a while now – ballet makes me feel graceful and strong. There's a lot to learn and I have to practise hard to build up my core strength and develop my technique. It's worth it though. I love the way ballet uses your whole body to express emotion and tell a story.

These dancers focus on their arm movements.

Classical

Classical ballet uses traditional ballet techniques. Because it was first developed in France, the steps and positions have French names. This type of ballet is very disciplined and formal. It relies on the legs being turned outwards from the hips to achieve precise yet flowing movement. Famous classical ballets include *The Nutcracker* and *Swan Lake*, with dances choreographed to music played by an orchestra.

Tamara Rojo and Carlos Acosta dance a duet, called a pas de deux.

Contemporary

Contemporary ballet is based on classical technique but with a broader range of movement and expression. Sometimes legs are turned in, and dancers may use off-centre shapes and body lines. Pointe work may be used, but not always; some contemporary ballet is performed barefoot. Costumes and music tend to be less traditional, too.

CHECKLIST

Ballet is based on five essential feet positions, known as first, second, third, fourth and fifth. Practising them helps develop the dancer's 'turnout' or correct leg position.

top ★ tip

En pointe is a technique used by more advanced dancers where they dance up on their toes, wearing specially reinforced ballet shoes. The shape this creates looks beautiful, but young dancers should not attempt pointe work until their feet are strong enough and their bones are properly formed.

Bhangra

Some of us in my class at school are working on a bhangra dance routine for our end-of-year show. We're using recorded music, though my friend's brother has offered to play the drums as well to make it extra special. We want to look as colourful as possible so we're making our own costumes. I can't wait!

A celebration

Like many dance styles, bhangra began as a folk dance in the Punjab region of India, to celebrate the harvest. The music is based on a fast drum beat and folk singing punctuated by cries such as 'hoi hoi!' It's a high energy style with lots of raised arm movements, foot hops and raised legs. Each sequence of movements on one side of the body is always mirrored or repeated by the same sequence on the opposite side. Dancers are usually barefoot.

The drum beat gives bhangra its distinctive rhythms.

Bollywood style

Nowadays the traditional bhangra style is often fused with western street dance styles. Dancers may perform it in formation, sometimes in quite large groups made popular by set-piece dances in Bollywood films. The music may also combine elements of pop or hip hop with the bhangra drum beat. Bhangra dancing competitions have become popular in many parts of the world.

These dancers wear loose-fitting salwar kameez.

CHECKLIST

For a traditional look, wear the following:

- ☑ Boys – turban, chaadra (piece of cloth wrapped around the legs) and kurta (a long shirt)

- ☑ Girls – salwar kameez (tunic and baggy trousers)

top tip

Arm, wrist and hand movements are emphasised in bhangra. Dancers swing their arms, shake their shoulders and circle their wrists, while fingers often make specific shapes. Let your eyes follow your hands as they move. Symmetry is important, too. Remember that an arm swing or sideways step or circling movement on one side of the body must always be repeated on the other side.

Irish step dancing

Dancing with hard shoes.

Irish step dancing looks amazing. I went to a ceili recently, which is where you do Irish social dancing, and I saw a display dance by a girl whose legs and feet moved so fast I couldn't even follow the steps! It's a bit like tap but with lots of jumps, hops and kicks. The other difference is that the dancers don't move their upper bodies. They hold their arms straight down by their sides.

Soft shoe and hard shoe

There are two kinds of Irish step dancing: 'soft shoe' and 'hard shoe'. In soft shoe, girls wear soft leather pumps with laces to hold them in place, and boys wear black shoes with fibreglass heels that they can click together. The hard shoe looks a bit like a bulky tap shoe. Both types use set dance patterns and traditional music based on folk reels and jigs.

Straight arms

The stiff, straight arms of Irish step dancers are very distinctive. Many people think it is because the dances developed in small homes and crowded rooms. The dancers didn't have space to swing their arms or move very far across the floor. Later on, judges at dance festivals approved because it meant they could focus on the intricate footwork of the competitors.

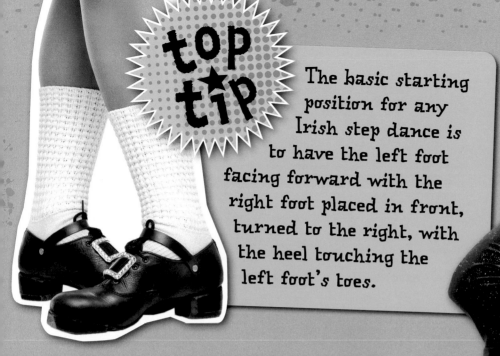

top tip

The basic starting position for any Irish step dance is to have the left foot facing forward with the right foot placed in front, turned to the right, with the heel touching the left foot's toes.

Dancing competitively

An Irish step dancing competition is called a 'feis', pronounced 'fash'. Dancers are judged mainly on the quality of their dancing, but also on how they present themselves. Boys wear black trousers and a smart shirt. Girls wear decorated dresses, white socks or tights and they are expected to have heavily curled hair. Most of them wear wigs!

THE EXPERT SAYS...

Irish dancer Michael Flatley whose *Riverdance* show popularised Irish dancing around the world has these words of advice for young dancers: "The most important thing is that you believe in yourself and keep on going."

Dance for life

Dancing is a huge part of my life. I dance on my own, with my friends, at dance classes and in shows and competitions. I know I've loads to learn but going to classes and practising afterwards is all part of the fun. Maybe I'll be a professional dancer one day, or maybe I'll just do it because I love it. Either way, I'll always be dancing!

Fit and happy

Dance allows you to keep fit, build up core strength, relax, be creative, have fun and make new friends – all at the same time! Plenty of other sports also contain dance elements: think of synchronised swimming, ice skating, rhythmic gymnastics and capoeira, which is a form of martial arts mixed with dance. All rely on expression as well as technical skill.

Capoeira is a fusion of martial arts and dance.

A flash mob dancing in the street.

Watch and do

There are so many different ways to enjoy dance. With your parents' permission, watch some clips on the Internet — great for learning basic steps and seeing how the experts do it. Sign up for dance classes, watch street dancers, go to a live performance to see some ballet or tap or simply dance around your bedroom. Get the beat and get moving!

top tip

A sponsored dance event such as a group line dance is a great way to raise money for charity and have fun at the same time. How about a sponsored 'moon walk' or a sponsored salsa?

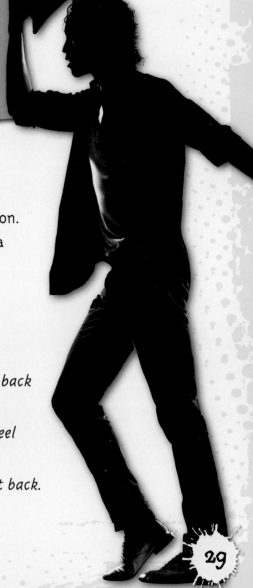

The moon walk

The moon walk is a crazy dance step made famous by Michael Jackson. It looks like you are gliding backwards! Practise it in your socks on a smooth floor.

★ *Feet together, facing forward.*

★ *Slide right foot back and raise heel up. Toes stay on the floor.*

★ *Let the right foot take your weight.*

★ *Slide left foot back, keeping heel on the floor until it is further back than your right foot.*

★ *Snap your left heel up, and at the same time snap your right heel down.*

★ *Now let the left foot take your weight and slide your right foot back.*

★ *Snap the right heel up and snap the left heel down.*

Now repeat!

Quiz

How mad about dance are you? Try this quiz and find out!

1. What's the point of warming up before you dance?

(a) To get you in the mood

(b) To help avoid injury

(c) To keep you busy while your teacher finds the right music

2. When is a ballet dancer ready for pointe work?

(a) When she or he is eleven

(b) When she or he has been dancing for at least three years

(c) When the dancer's mentally prepared and their feet are strong enough

3. What is a syncopated rhythm?

(a) A rhythm that emphasises the off-beat

(b) A regular rhythm

(c) A fast rhythm

4. What is the most important element in Irish step dancing?

(a) A distinctive costume and wig

(b) The movement of the arms

(c) Foot work

5. What does a choreographer do?

(a) Advise dancers on their technique

(b) Design a dance sequence or create a new dance

(c) Design the dance costumes

6. What is b-boying?

(a) Beat boxing

(b) Bouncing up and down

(c) Breakdancing

7. In a salsa dance step, which part of the body touches the floor first?

(a) The ball of the foot

(b) The toes

(c) The heel of the foot

8. Why is it important to see yourself in a mirror during a dance class?

(a) To make sure you aren't going to bump into anyone

(b) To make sure your hair is tied back neatly at all times

(c) To check your body alignment and position

Answers:
1(b); 2(c); 3(a); 4(c); 5(b); 6(c); 7(a); 8(c)

Glossary

a cappella dancing or singing without musical accompaniment.

ballet a formal, disciplined form of dancing characterised by legs turned out and dancing on the tips of the feet.

ballroom a wide variety of partner dances; one partner leads and the other follows.

bhangra fast and lively Indian dance style.

body popping a street dance style where parts of the body appear to jerk briefly.

breakdancing a freestyle dance form associated with hip hop music.

cha cha a Latin ballroom dance style based on a triple step of right-left-right.

choreography designing dance moves and putting them together in a set sequence.

downrocking hip hop moves where the dancer's shoulders are close to the floor and the body is supported by the hands.

en pointe where ballet dancers wearing block shoes dance on the tips of their feet.

formation where couples dance in patterns with other couples.

foxtrot a smooth, elegant ballroom dance, similar to the waltz.

freestyle a style of popular dancing where the dancer makes up the sequence of moves.

freeze poses hip hop moves where the body is held still in a balance.

grapevine a sequence of steps that causes the dancer to move in a figure of eight.

hip hop a style of dance that developed with hip hop music in New York in the 1970s.

improvised dance sequences or moves that are made up by the dancers during a dance.

jig a lively folk dance tune.

jive a form of Latin ballroom dancing with a lively, syncopated rhythm.

krumping an expressive and energetic style of street dance.

line dancing a line of dancers doing the same steps at the same time.

locking freezing from a fast movement and holding a pose before continuing with another fast movement.

macarena a popular line dance with easy-to-learn moves.

paso doble a Latin ballroom dance style that began in Spain.

quickstep an upbeat ballroom dance.

samba a Latin ballroom dance style that began in Brazil.

salsa a popular and upbeat social dance in which weight changes from foot to foot.

signature move a move that is closely associated with a particular dancer.

syncopated an unexpected rhythm, one that emphasises the off-beat.

tango a highly expressive ballroom partner dance that began in Argentina.

waltz an elegant, gliding ballroom dance.

Index